echoes
from
an
island

a woman's search

short stories and poems by
ALICIA ANG

For my family,

my tree of love.

The most beautiful things in the world cannot be seen
or touched, they are felt with the heart.

THE LITTLE PRINCE

Antoine de Saint-Exupéry

The world is too small to live in one place only.

contents

∞

introduction

∞

Will you chase a dream?

An art print on Etsy caught my eye back in April 2018. It was of an ocean wave that struck me as aspirational, serene, and calm. Right away I ordered it, framed it, and hung it on my bedroom wall so that I would see it every morning when I woke up. I'd imagine hearing the waves crash against the shore while digging my feet into the warm sand. I knew I longed for a sweet escape. I was seeking something.

If it is a blur, will you still seek it?

Back then, I had little clarity in my life, barely a vision of *the thing* I sought. However, I knew that I had to explore. One day in February 2019, I woke up with a jolt. There was a sudden urgency in me to travel, and it was going to be a long one. I would miss the chance if I did not allow myself to venture boldly. I tried to pinpoint my goal. I envisioned my wildest dreams, and it was to do animation, much like Pixar and Disney, except in Chinese and rooted in Chinese culture. But I wasn't certain about that either. Nevertheless, I founded an animation studio, Dream Factory Stories Pte Ltd., and found the courage to uproot myself from my home in Singapore.

I bought a one-way ticket to China, traveling through all my favorite cities and discovering several new ones. The sights and sounds from my travels allowed me to develop several story ideas. I started in Beijing at my alma mater, Peking University. Thereafter, I journeyed to Xi'an via high-speed rail. From Xi'an, I traveled down south to Chengdu and Chongqing. Finally, I ended my first leg of travel in Xiamen, my ancestral home.

I returned to Beijing soon after, staying at my friend's hutong house. There, I unexpectedly chanced upon a WeChat post that detailed a call by the Singapore Business Federation for Singaporean business owners to participate in an overseas market workshop in China. I signed up for it, and the next thing I knew, I was visiting tech companies in Hong Kong and Shenzhen, heavily networking with other business owners, and seeking inputs for Dream Factory.

Upon hearing my aspirations, a business delegate from the workshop connected me to the Singaporean business and creative communities in Shanghai. In

Shanghai, while we were in talks of putting up a musical, I was also paying visits to producers and mentors in Singapore and Taiwan to work out my animation company ideas. But despite my efforts, I was not getting any closer to my envisioned goal. Animation may not have been the path I was seeking after all. I was receiving heartfelt advice from mentors too, but I was so early on my path to understanding them then. For example, a mentor advised me to "soak in a place" and to "go as deep as I can to uncover human nature." Another mentor shared that I needed "the precipitation of life and culture." These words perplexed me incessantly for a while.

If you do not find what you were seeking, will you continue the journey?
Eventually, I decided to take a piece of advice from a mentor to explore other countries. I told myself I would circle back to China. I planned on Japan, Mongolia, and Russia. My first stop: a four-day stay in Okinawa, Japan.

It was a hot summer night in July when I finally reached Okinawa. Surprisingly, I felt a connection to the place very quickly. By the third day, I was extending my stay and canceling all my bookings for Mongolia and Russia. I enjoyed the beaches, the Okinawa Churaumi Aquarium, the heritage sites and museums, the old streets, the cafes, and especially the food. It was everything, the wanderlust in me, love. In the next two weeks, I learned that Okinawa was once a four hundred fifty-year-old island-state known as the Ryukyu kingdom. Chinese, Japanese, and Southeast Asian cultures influenced its evolution. There were unforeseen similarities with my home country, Singapore, as well. Intuitively, I started working on an Okinawan story. I was thrilled.

Then I had the idea of spending half a year in Shanghai to pursue other creative ventures, and the other half in Okinawa to write my story. But within a few weeks, I knew I had to choose one and commit fully. There was this uncanny belief I held that henceforth for an extended period, I would not be able to travel as freely as before. And so, I decided to follow my heart and chose to write the story.

And so, it begins

In October 2019, I enrolled as a language student at a Japanese language school in Naha, the prefectural capital of Okinawa. My routine was straightforward: Four hours of writing at the library, lunch, and then school. My free time was spent enjoying Okinawa and soaking in everything she had to offer.

I was writing a huge YA historical fantasy that spanned multiple eras and places. My protagonist began as a refugee in Okinawa after her dynasty fell in China. It was bleak and depressing.

Over time, world events and my personal growth reshaped my story.

On Halloween 2019, a fire destroyed Shuri Castle, a key Gusuku site of the nine sites registered under the UNESCO World Heritage Site and the cultural symbol of Okinawa. It was unnerving even for a visitor. Not to mention, I could no longer experience or investigate the castle for my writing. What felt so permanent was destroyed in a single night of flames.

Soon after, the Covid-19 pandemic hit the world and changed it irrevocably. In Okinawa, the tourists left, events were canceled, and the streets became empty. I was afraid to catch Covid because I hardly spoke Japanese then. Okinawa changed, the world changed, and it felt more depressing than the story I was writing. I sought online therapy from SACAC Counselling to deal with my stresses and to learn to "leave my worlds" when I put my pen down.

After collecting enough material from museums, books, pamphlets, and historical site visits, I was ready to study them for my story. This singular step took me a year or so because I could only write a story about Okinawa if I became an expert on it. However, just as I finished compiling the content into my Macbook, it crashed, and I threw in the towel. It was too much to bear! I decided to give up this dream and focus on getting a job.

Reset at 30

After several anxious months of waiting to hit thirty, I hit it, and right after that, I found myself giving little or no care to milestones that I thought I should hit by thirty. I decided to learn from other writers and give writing another go.

For a start, I signed up for MasterClass. I gained confidence and discovered my feminine voice from attending classes of established female writers, namely Joy Harjo and Amy Tan. I also learned I had inferiority complexes within myself that I was unaware of, hindering me from my pursuits. Most importantly, I gained awareness of my voice as a Singaporean Chinese female writer.

With that, I found the courage to write again. This time, I switched from writing in Chinese to English, infused what I learned from NFTs, and decided to test my stories on a blog, metasparks.blog. I watched my writing evolve and the rawness and essence of who I was coming out of me. I was developing my voice and honing my craft.

I closed Dream Factory and let go of my epic YA historical fantasy. With a newfound space and lightness, I found myself weaving memories, travel sights and sounds, and contemplations of home into my writing. I went back to the sites and used the information I could find online to build up my story. My characters and stories were interweaving. Yet again, I lost confidence and stopped writing. There was this nagging worry about money. How was writing stories going to feed me?

The missing ingredient

In September 2022, I decided to hire a life coach to get my life in order. In other words, to stay away from my daydreaming once and for all. Ironically, the work with my life coach had me finishing my manuscript and designing a book cover by the end of October. I am already contemplating stories for my next book.

I realized I have the fire to chase down my dreams, to turn them into reality. But I lacked the immovable strength and clarity of purpose. Apart from venturing out, I needed to seek my *why* from within me, an introspection that required stillness, surrender, and attentiveness —almost the opposite of traits when venturing out. Once I knew my *why*, I gained powerful momentum to carry me to the finishing line.

Echoes from an Island

This collection comprises four sections. The first four poems are in "26.2170° N, 127.7195° E," the geographic coordinates of Okinawa. The following short stories are found in "Oki Times." They can be read independently or as a trilogy. The first story, "The Moon Princess," tells the mythical journey of a Ming Chinese Princess in the seventeen century to the Ryukyu kingdom. The second story, "Travel Fortune," is set in present-day Okinawa and recounts the adventures of a traveler with a local Okinawan grandma. The third story, "Metaland," is set in 2063 and tells the quest of a daughter trying to reconnect with and revive her dying mother via the metaverse. These short stories are then followed by two poems grouped under the header of

"The Shimmering Moon on Howling Nights," sharing chaotic thoughts that float up to consciousness deep in the night. Finally, the collection ends with "Parting Words."

Gems don't burn away

Today is Culture Day, a public holiday in Japan. Over the weekend, a long tree trunk was trucked south from the northern Yambaru National Park. This morning, on a hot autumn day, it arrived at Shuri Castle with a procession to officiate the rebuilding of the castle. Events at the site followed, and I was there basking in the atmosphere with the crowd.

Now, as I look out at my balcony this evening, I can see the nearby Shuri Castle. I can also see the horizon where the sky kisses the ocean. It reminds me of my ocean wave print.

I hope you enjoy this collection of poems and short stories. I hope you hear the island whispers that I hear, taste the slice of sub-urban island life that I savor, and see the layers of Okinawa that I see as a visitor of this magical island.

Alicia Ang

November 3, 2022

Shuri, Okinawa

26.2170° N, 127.7195° E

∞

echoes from an island

alicia ang

gliding planes

I live where the ocean blends with the sky,
where islands float on ethereal blue,
where large breezy clouds drift me by.
Islands of the Ryukyus,
this is Okinawa.

From my place,
I can see the silent ascend of planes across the horizon.
Like a gliding sea creature in her steady course,
she knows intuitively where to roam.

Did I mention my cat and I like to watch the sunset?
Oh yes, she is part of the magic around me.
Sometimes, we catch it at the corner of our eyes,
builders rebuilding the Shuri Castle.
Like Lego men on Lego blocks,
they dangle on ropes,
hard at work.

I wonder what she thinks of what she sees.

Tell me now, what magic do you see?
Tell me all about it.
I want to know.
Capture them with words,
draw them if you must.
Send me them all,
I want to see them with your eyes.

Catch my well-wishes from the incoming plane
to your place.
Send me cargo full of kisses and love notes.
Throw in a bouquet of flowers too.
I want magic to reach you.
I want to receive magic.
I want them all to encircle our world.

there is a little grave near where I live

There is a little grave near where I live.
At a corner of a slope,
marked by a carefully chopped tree,
it sits alone.

I used to be scared of graves.
I don't really see them from where I come from.
They are separated from the living,
and I had all these imaginations about them.

But once during a school trip to Scotland,
I visited an old churchyard.
As I observed the gravestone of Adam Smith,
I wasn't quite sure if I should've been afraid.

This reminds me of the Cemetery in Singapore.
Elaborate and sprawling,
a hundred thousand graves,
so close to my once family home,
yet so hidden and unknown to me.

I only discovered it in my mid-twenties.
Is it still there?

They call it Bukit Brown,
and I often imagine the deceased
all decked out in their glorious final wear,
having a little tea party of sorts.

I often wonder if they
-these unexpected migrants from faraway shores-
could speak to one another.

The truth is,
there's a family of graves near where I live too.
But they don't catch my attention as much.

Wait,
that little grave I mentioned earlier
is not a grave.
It's a shrine!

Why did I remember it as a grave?

It is a lone shrine by a chopped tree,

with an NTT Docomo tower

erected right next to it.

They say that where I live was a spiritual place.

Prayers and blessings were made

to watch over the nearby castle and its rulers.

But there are no more rulers.

The castle ground is now a UNESCO site.

Who then comes to pray and sweep the steps to the

shrine?

echoes from the ocean, yuta of the islands

The spirit kisses the mutable sand,
and chisels the calcareous rocks on every strand.
Sweeping across the Ryukyu Islands,
it hunts for a match with a soon-to-be *yuta*.

Not by blood or by will or whim,
the spirit chooses her; she lets it in.
A union, a psychic awakening of she who then shells
herself,
like a hermit crab that is amongst others
but truly alone.

A *yuta* speaks to all who seek echoes from the ocean.
No, she cannot be self-serving.
But she too can be lost in the eye of a hurricane.
After all, she is not a god.

One day, as with all waters flowing back to the ocean,
the spirit will retreat.
She knows, but she can only see it go away.
Leaving her, the hermit,
only with her torn, weathered shell.

someone I met

Like many of us, she is not of this land.
I look into her eyes,
her large pupils with an awful lot of white
stare back at me.
Beneath her loosely draped wear,
fashioned with hidden pins,
I could see a strength in that
slightly hunched, thin frame of hers.

She needed no jewelry to adorn her.
She needed no tailored wear to fashion her.
She had no makeup or perfume to refine her.
She had no oversized leather bag or fancy heels to
elevate her.
Yet, she is beautiful.

I was in awe.
I could never be like her.
Or could I?
Could I make the choices that she made,
endure the journeys that she took to get here?
Could I be like her in similar circumstances?

All she has is forged by her sweat and hands.
She is not much older,
but I felt her spirit.
It is young, exhausted, but strong.

It is the Human Spirit that I've felt.
It endures and lives in all of us.
She is, without a doubt,
someone who I have had the honor to have met.

oki times

∞

echoes from an island

alicia ang

the moon princess

1.

In April 1644, when rebels approached the Chinese capital, the Ming Emperor Chongzhen slew his kin and hung himself from a tree. This set in motion for China to complete her cyclical passage of a dynasty collapsing to a dynasty birthing. It is then the tale of a girl, a princess whose life changed from the collapse of her dynasty, begins.

This is the tale of the Moon Princess who left an imprint beyond her time.

2.

April 1644

Forbidden City, Beijing, China

"Wake up, Moon! Ming is collapsing. The rebels have entered the outer palace. Swallow the Flaming Pearl and leave at once. Quickly now, hurry!"

With trembling hands, Concubine Shun fed her daughter, Moon, the Pearl. Then, carefully, with a thin golden blade, she cut Moon's thumb and dripped her blood on a palm-sized bronze creature statue.

She assured them both, "This will protect you. You need not be afraid. There is no time to be afraid."

Bang! The doors flew open to reveal a disheveled

man in golden robes. It was Emperor Chongzhen. Defeated and downcast, he dragged his blood-stained golden sword toward them.

"I'm sorry… I'm so sorry…This will all end now…."

Concubine Shun flung herself in front of a shell-shocked Moon. Without warning, the emperor pierced his sword into Concubine Shun's heart. Moon screamed and fainted on the back of an approaching creature. Like a fierce howling wind, it carried Moon away from the burning palace and into the capital.

When Moon woke up, she realized the creature that saved her was the bronze statue that came to life at the drop of her blood. It was the legendary protector, Qi Bao Pi. A deer-like being with cyan scales armoring its torso, it had antlers on its crown and long white whiskers circling its mouth. She thought of her mother and felt as though she was drowning in a deep, dark well.

Barely pausing for rest, Qi Bao Pi ran as far away from the capital as it could. It brought Moon deep into the forest where no rebels could reach them. Yet, slowly but surely, the relentless rebels, and later the Qing army, which would cement themselves as the new rulers of China, combed through every forest and mountain in search of surviving Ming loyalists. At last, the pair was forced to flee to the southern coastal areas.

"Where can I go? Nowhere in China is safe for me."

Qi Bao Pi carried her further south to the southern caves by the southernmost port. For the first time, Moon smelled the saltiness of the ocean breeze.

By a stream of water leading to the ocean, Qi Bao Pi sang into a large spiral seashell. Gently, a hundred-year-old hibernating turtle awakened and broke free from within the cave walls. He smiled at Moon and his old friend, Qi Bao Pi.

The Pearl in Moon shone, and the turtle obeyed. With the guidance of the Pearl, the turtle carried Moon and Qi Bao Pi across the Eastern Sea.

When the trio arrived at the Ryukyu kingdom, the Ming dynasty officially ended with the Qing Emperor Shunzhi ruling over China. The Moon Princess had lost her home.

3.

The turtle left when Moon and Qi Bao Pi arrived onshore. At Naha harbor, the gentle waves rocked the junk boats while children played by the shallow waters. Situated by the cliffs, soft light from the Nami-no-ue Shrine colored the scene with warm illumination.

At the docks, an old woman in white was waiting for Moon. She was a *yuta*, a spirit medium. She walked toward

Moon and said, "You are grieving. Come with me."

Moon was uncertain, but she knew the *yuta* could give Moon what she needed, so she followed her.

The *yuta* led them into a cave not far from the harbor. She offered them some water and food. And then, she said, "You have what I want. The Flaming Pearl from the Ancients that protects she who consumes it. Without the Pearl, you would have perished with your kingdom."

Moon had no fear of death, for she did not feel deserving of survival.

"I will give you what you want in exchange for the Pearl."

"You can't. No one can give me what I yearn for."

"I can show you your mother."

"I will give anything to see Ma."

"Wait," Qi Bao Pi cautioned, "Without the Pearl, you are open to all dangers."

Teary-eyed, Moon offered her protector a curt smile and replied, "I will give anything to see Ma."

With that, the *yuta* laid Moon down and closed her eyes. She chanted and gently touched Moon's forehead. Slowly, a blurry vision formed and came into focus. Moon cried. A young girl, barely twelve, appeared before her. She had a beautiful oval face with almond-shaped eyes. It was, without a doubt, Ma. Ma smiled at Moon. With the strength of the rolling tide, emotions crashed into Moon and left her in a flood of tears. But all too soon, Ma morphed into a black butterfly and fluttered away.

"Ma!" Moon opened her eyes and cried, "That was her!"

"She was always by your side. She was waiting to bid you farewell."

"I want to see her again."

"No. Not anymore. And now, my Flaming Pearl."

The *yuta* commenced her chant. The Pearl in Moon's chest shone as it yielded to its new mistress.

4.

Moon found herself in a humid cave with a faint light peering in from the outside. Her head was heavy, her throat was dry, and her body was cold.

The chant-like dripping sound gave away the presence of long stalactites hanging above her. With every painful move of her muscles, she pulled herself across the cave until she felt the taste of water. She lay there, mouth agape until she passed out again.

∞

In a barely conscious state, Moon heard an exchange between two men. They were in the cave, somewhere closer to the entrance.

"How many units are available for purchase?"

"As many as you want."

"I'll take a hundred units first. If everything goes well, we can do ten thousand units… quarterly."

"Deal. In the next shipment, your men will find a hundred units at Manila harbor."

"Send my regards to your father. I hope he gets well soon."

With a quivering voice, the younger man replied, "Thank you."

As footsteps quietened, Moon fell back into unconsciousness.

Qi Bao Pi fed Moon sea algae till she regained her strength. And though she had given up the Pearl to the *yuta*, in return, the parting with Ma gave Moon back her spirit. It was as if the thick black fog that had consumed her since Ma's death had finally dissipated, and she could breathe again. Ma was dead. But Ma would always live in her.

With Qi Bao Pi by her side, she pulled herself together and walked out of the cave. With the guidance of the morning sun, she slowly traced the winding beach. Faint sounds grew louder; soft lights grew brighter. She followed them and found herself in a sprawling marketplace.

5.

The marketplace was brimming with life. There were at least eight alleys of sellers. Underneath umbrellas that were barely shading them from the scorching sun, the sellers beckoned for passersby to make purchases. One could see an assortment of vegetables, tofu, and potatoes in one alley. In another alley, one could smell seafood, pig's broth, and the Ryukyuan spirit, *awamori*. The locals spoke a language that Moon could not comprehend. She noticed they had tattoo motifs on their hands too and wondered what they meant.

A local woman with her food supported on her head caught Moon's attention. She was bargaining hard with a seemingly upset seller. Amused, she watched the scene until she realized Qi Bao Pi was nowhere beside her.

She searched around for it anxiously. She walked through the streets of fishmongers and meat sellers until she reached a shallow harbor that had a few wooden boats bobbing along with the rhythmic waves. She sat by the harbor for a rest when out came from the waters a magnificent sea giant.

The sea giant had an overly large head with gill slits on his body and webbed fingers and toes. He had a gentle smile, which made Moon naturally at ease with him. He walked towards Moon and asked, "Are you the Ming Princess with the Flaming Pearl? The entire Eastern Sea knows of your escape from China to Ryukyu."

"Oh! Yes, I am. I mean… I was."

"Oh?"

"I am no longer a princess, and I no longer possess the Flaming Pearl."

"Oh."

Puzzled, Moon asked, "Why are you looking for me?"

"I was hoping you could bring my family back."

"How?"

"Don't you know? By using the Pearl, it can bring the dead back to life."

"Really?"

"Yes. At least, that's what my brother told me before he was turned into an ocean stone."

"I'm sorry about your brother."

"It's alright, it happened a hundred years ago, along with everyone else."

"Everyone else? You mean your family?"

"Yes. My family and the entire tribe actually. I am the only one left after the attack of the *irabu*."

"What's an *irabu*?"

"It is a black-banded venomous sea snake. It's a small but horrible creature. I pray you never meet one."

"The Flaming Pearl is with a *yuta* now… Can the Pearl really bring the dead back to life?"

"I think so. Do you remember what the *yuta* looks like?"

"I do."

"I say we go find her and get the Flaming Pearl back. It is worth a try, at the very least."

Moon hesitated, but she knew the sea giant was right. She did not want to see the sea giant going back to the ocean alone as well. If the Pearl could resurrect the dead, maybe it could help find Qi Bao Pi too. And so, Moon looked up at the sea giant, and for the first time in a long while, she *smiled*.

travel fortune

1.

July 2019

Gulangyu, an island off the southern coast of China

Hidden on a narrow alley of red brick buildings, away from the crowds on the main streets, was a cafe with three carefully placed seats. A young woman of no more than thirty was sitting quietly in the center seat, planning her next adventure. She studied the regional map on her iPad as she took another mouthful of her chai latte. Her eyes sparkled, wandered, and roamed. Korea? Japan? How about Mongolia? Hmm, or maybe westwards?

She couldn't decide, and that made her ecstatic. Finally, she rested her eyes on the owner, Lili, who was concentrating on her latte art. A wing appeared, and then another, and then a tiny head with a handsome body and long tail. She smiled. She has created something worthy, something tasteful.

Lynn proclaimed in Chinese, "*Piao liang!*"

"You really think it's beautiful?"

"Of course it is! Now tell me, where do you think I should go next?"

"Let me see… you want to stay in China or

somewhere else?"

Lynn exclaimed, "I've been in China for quite some time now. I am so ready for somewhere else."

"Seoul?"

"Been there."

"Busan?"

"Been there too."

"Jeju Island?"

"What for? Only honeymooners go there. I know you love Korea but how about somewhere else?"

"Well, how about Mongolia then? I remember you wanted to go see the Naadam Festival."

"Good idea! No, wait, if I'm going to Mongolia, I'd want to do a two-week kind of thing. It's too expensive for me to go right now. It's out of my budget."

Just then, a pair of Japanese tourists entered the cafe and ordered takeaways.

When they left, Lynn threw her hands up in the air with joy, "It's a sign! Japan it is!"

Lili rolled her eyes. Just as she went back to practicing her latte art, she suggested, "How about Okinawa? It's the nearest to where we are and probably the cheapest to get to. Many of my friends have been there for holidays, and they found the place…interesting. It's Japanese yet very Southeast Asian. Also, a bit like

Fujian and Taiwan too."

Lynn liked the sound of that. She searched for Okinawa on Google Maps, did a quick read-up on the location, checked for air tickets and accommodations, and beamed.

Next stop: *Okinawa.*

2.

July 2019

Shuri Castle, Okinawa

As Lynn walked out of the castle site, she skillfully took a selfie with the vermillion buildings peeking out from the stone walls. She spent some time cropping and adjusting its lighting.

Happy with the photo, she shared it on her social media accounts with the caption:

First day in #Okinawa and already visited this beautiful
#UNESCO site!

The old palace of the once Ryukyu kingdom~
Love it! #ShuriCastle

Check out my Tik Tok for a virtual tour of the castle

As she contemplated on the hashtags to add to her post, she wondered if she should finally call home. She decided to get a drink, and her earlier thought was swiftly forgotten. Her eyes searched the area, skipping past crowded gift shops and touristy cafes until she caught sight of a vending machine across the street. While making her way toward it, she fished from her coin pouch a one-hundred yen coin, and contemplated if she should have a bottle of cold water or *oolong* tea. She inserted the coin and pressed for cold water. Down fell the bottle, and with it came an unexpected beeping sound. She was caught off guard and wondered if she could have made a mistake during her purchase. In her limited understanding of Japanese, she tried to read the message on the vending machine screen, and to her amazement, as she was the seven thousand, seven hundred, and seventy-seventh customer of this vending machine, she won a free drink of her choice. Without hesitation, she pressed for *oolong* tea and was exuberant to share it on her social media.

Downing the bottle of icy cold water, she made her way down a couple of stone steps across from the vending machine and threw herself and her backpack onto a bench. She was planning her route to the guesthouse, when she noticed a large, black butterfly fluttering aimlessly around her. Her eyes followed it, and it flew behind her, and up the stone steps from where she came down from.

"HAI-YA!" An old lady steadied herself on the stone steps and swished and swashed her net several times in her attempt to catch the butterfly. Though the old lady was nimble, she was not quick enough to get hold of the little creature. Soon enough, it flew further up and disappeared. Still, the old lady was relentless. She waited, and in a minute, the butterfly came back. She smiled and waited for the butterfly to come closer. It tactfully landed on a tree branch, visible yet unreachable. It was mocking the old lady.

"Don't just stare! Lift me up!"

Lynn looked around, and there was no one else but her and the old lady.

"You! Yes, I am speaking to you! Come lift me up!"

Lynn hurried towards the old lady who was barely half her height. She steadied herself as carefully as she could on the steps and hoisted the old lady onto her shoulders.

"Get closer to the tree! Closer! Yes! HAI-YA! WE GOT IT!"

The old lady caught the butterfly with one swish of her net. But in the process of coming down off Lynn's shoulders, the butterfly escaped.

"Hmm…" The old lady pouted and panted, "Can't be helped…"

Lynn knew she should not stare, but she found the whole scene amusing, and she laughed heartily. The old lady smiled too. She asked, "What's your name? Where were you born?"

"I'm Lynn, and I am from Singapore."

"Lynn-san, *Haisai.*"

"I'm sorry?"

"That means *hello* in Okinawan."

"Oh, right! *Haisai!*"

Seeing the old lady panting from her butterfly chase, she offered her the bottle of *oolong* tea.

"Thank you, but no thanks."

"How may I address you?"

"You can call me Kinjo."

"*Haisai*, Kinjo-san! It's nice to meet you."

"You speak very good Japanese."

"Ohh, no, no I don't."

"Have you eaten? Would you like some tea and dessert? I live just over there."

Lynn felt at ease around Kinjo-san. And so, she smiled widely, and in polite Japanese, she agreed and followed her home.

3.

Kinjo-san's house was in one of the small alleys running across the stone steps. It was a fairly large two-story house with a spectacular garden. It had blooming hibiscus, bougainvillea, and many local plants Lynn did not recognize. As with all other buildings in Okinawa, a pair of dog-like stone statues flanked the wooden gates.

Kinjo-san looked at them and said, "*Shisa*, guardian creatures. Some English-speaking people call them 'shisa dogs,' but they are not dogs, more like lions."

Lynn nodded and smiled sheepishly while the traveler in her knew for sure then that Kinjo-san was to be her helpful local friend throughout her stay here. The type who would feed hungry travelers, drive them all over town and act as local guides at the "must-go" tourist sites. In fact, a little out of the ordinary, even for hospitable Japanese, she may suggest housing her new traveler friends for a day or two.

"Wow, these are-"

"Family stuff."

"Really? Wow. It looks like a museum."

Upon entering Kinjo-san's home, Lynn was greeted with a doorway full of antiques. She could not tell if Kinjo-san was an avid collector or someone who discarded nothing. There were tea sets, scrolls of paintings and calligraphy, vases, furniture, and textiles. Many of which would sit nicely together with the exhibits in the castle that she had visited earlier. Lynn hugged her backpack and carefully walked into the house. As she walked further in, she could not help but wonder about Kinjo-san's life.

"If you are interested, I can share many stories with you. But first, let's eat."

Kinjo-san walked out of the kitchen with a plateful of sweet *chinbin*, decorated with pineapple, mango, berries, and a glass of chilled *sanpin-cha*. It was as if she knew she would be expecting a guest today.

"These are delicious. Thank you."

"How long are you staying in Okinawa?"

"Four days."

"Where are you staying?"

"At the Goya Guesthouse near Kenchomae."

"Nice place. Where are you looking to visit?"

"Well, today is my first day, and I've visited Shuri Castle. It was wonderful. I plan to visit the shopping street Kokusai Dori tomorrow and then maybe a beach in the evening. The reviews for the Prefectural Museum are great, so I think I will go there too. Actually, do you, by any chance, know where I should visit?"

"Let's walk Kokusai Dori tomorrow. There are many hidden gems behind the main street that only I know."

"Ah, but you mustn't. I have troubled you too much already."

"No, no, I insist. In fact, let's grab a bowl of *Okinawa soba* now before I send you to your guesthouse. I am sure you will like it. It is very different. Do you like pig feet? There is a restaurant in Kenchomae that sells very yummy pig feet."

No longer intending to be polite, Lynn replied, "Oh! No! No! You shouldn't! I can make my way to the guesthouse! Really! And you have fed me delicious *chinbin* and *sanpin-cha* already!"

"No, no, I insist. Let's go now. I'll see you in the car."

Lynn knew there was no use resisting her new friend, so she quickly downed her last bit of *sapin-cha* and grabbed her backpack. As she looked around the house one final time, she noticed at the far corner of the living room table sat a carefully displayed photograph. In that photo were Kinjo-san and a woman who looked like a younger version of her. They smiled proudly without revealing a single tooth. With them stood a Caucasian man and a pair of biracial children. Family stuff.

Next to the photo placed a tiny frame, and it enclosed a painting of a woman in a faded pink *hanfu*.

Her melancholic eyes gazed at a seemingly faraway land. A Chinese woman? At that moment, Lynn felt a tug in her heart and stared at the painting intently once more.

4.

Lynn and Kinjo-san were enjoying their Blue Seal ice creams in a well-packed café. Kinjo-san had arrived at eight in the morning to pick Lynn up from the guesthouse. By noon, they had finished walking most of Kokusai Dori and the markets behind. Along the way, Lynn picked up a pair of *shisa* painted in bright red and orange. They tasted dried local seafood, desserts, fruits, and *mozuku*, a slimy and refreshingly sour seaweed shaped like angel hair pasta. As Lynn contemplated the next stop, she savored the cookie and cream off her tiny wooden spoon and proceeded to scratch the patch of eczema at the back of her left ear.

"What's that?"

Lynn flipped back her ear to reveal a patch of flushed skin. She brushed it off as a helpless situation that surfaced during her travels in the southwest part of China. Though secretly, she viewed her eczema as the proud battle scars of a seasoned traveler.

"I think it was in Guangxi that my eczema first appeared, or was it Wuxi? Can't really recall. But anyway, there are some on my elbows and back too."

"Have you seen a doctor?"

"Yeah. But it comes and goes, and it doesn't fully go away."

"Well, we'll get it treated today."

Lynn was skeptical but was curious for Kinjo-san to lead the way. Despite her tiny frame, Kinjo-san had a way of evoking command. Perhaps it was this trait of Kinjo-san that reminded Lynn of her late grandmother.

The pair took the car and made their way to the nearby Kainan Street. Kinjo-san parked by the road curb and led Lynn through the busy street. A waft of familiarity sent Lynn straight into a panic.

"We are going for TCM?"

"What's TCM?"

"We call it TCM back home. It means Traditional Chinese medicine."

"Yes, TCM. You got your eczema in China, so we treat it at its root."

A sizable stand-up banner greeted the pair. Three bold kanji characters were printed. *Kanpo yaku*. *Kanpo* for short. Han medicine from China before China became present-day China.

"Wait, is this a Japanese Chinese medicine hall? Or is it a Chinese-run, Chinese medicine hall?"

"Just come inside."

The wooden hand-painted plaque board and rows of herbs in the display window concealed the contemporary interiors of the medicine hall. As the pair waited in the tea area, they overheard a conversation in the examination room. An anxious Chinese lady who spoke with a northern accent relied on her bilingual Chinese friend to communicate with the practitioner.

"If you are concerned, you should not take my medicine."

"She is just a little concerned because you prescribed a weaker dosage compared to what she is used to having from other places."

"In my opinion, this is enough for her."

"Okay. My friend would like to know if she can continue her Western medicine."

"It is best to not mix the two. If your friend insists, she should have a two-hour interval between medicines."

Lynn was surprised. These were common questions even for TCM practitioners, *sinsehs*, back home in Singapore.

"Thank you. We will take our leave."

As the pair walked out of the examination room, Kinjo-san led Lynn in to see the physician. For one reason or another, be it TCM or *kanpo*, the practitioner tended to be a man in his fifties or sixties. And indeed, in sat a man in his fifties or sixties.

Kinjo-san and the practitioner, Nago-sensei, exchanged friendly greetings and spoke in a mix of heavy-accented Japanese and the local dialect. They were longtime friends. Kinjo-san explained Lynn's condition, and Nago-sensei carefully examined Lynn's eczema.

When done, he addressed them both in simple Japanese, "I will need time to prepare. Come back in an hour to make payment and collect your medicine."

Lynn was a little anxious and asked, "How much will it be?"

"It's the standard fee of six hundred yen for a day's worth of medicine, and you will need thirty days' worth for a start."

Lynn was bewildered. She would have to find some work to pay for the medicine. Noticing Lynn's worry, Kinjo-san offered to pay, which Lynn immediately refused.

"How are you going to pay if I don't help?"

"I'm going to work at the guesthouse. If they would take me."

"So you are staying longer?"

"Yes, I am. At least until I have finished my course

of medicine."

Kinjo-san beamed.

"Let's go eat taco rice. It's like a taco but without the shells on rice, and you can add lots of cheese and sauces. Or how about a Spam and egg *onigiri*? Tonight, we drink Okinawan alcohol, *awamori*, and fried pig skin at my place."

"Isn't the diet of the Okinawans supposed to be really clean and healthy? That's the reason for the longevity of the Okinawans, no? Like only root vegetables, tofu, seaweed, and grains?"

Kinjo-san laughed boisterously till onlookers smiled at them with amusement.

"Commercial bullshit."

A few onlookers stared at Kinjo-san.

"There are many kinds of Okinawans."

5.

It was Lynn's third week in Okinawa, and she was surprised to find herself still inquisitive about the place. On this day, Lynn was helping Kinjo-san clean her antiques when Kinjo-san asked about Lynn's travels.

"I've been traveling for close to two years now, and nope, I've not gone home in between. I mean, I do miss home from time to time, but I enjoy being out of the country."

"What do your parents think?"

"They just let me be; I mean, what can they do? I'm twenty-six! I'm so old already."

"You're twenty-six? I'm eighty-two."

"No way! You look so young and energetic."

"It's the pigskin and tobacco, trust me."

"What about you, Kinjo-san? Do you like to travel?"

"Oh, not really. I get seasick and airsick! It's just not in me to travel."

As Kinjo-san pulled herself up from the ground, she noticed Lynn's slender arms and compared them with her thick arms. She laughed and walked to the bathroom, "Don't grow old, okay?"

Lynn wondered what that meant for a second and continued to clean Kinjo-san's scrolls and teapots. As a result of Kinjo-san's meticulous care, the antiques in Kinjo-san's place were well-maintained.

"You will tell me some stories, won't you?"

"Hmm, what do you want to know?"

Lynn randomly picked up a large wooden box and asked, "What's inside?"

Kinjo-san put down her cigarette and carefully opened the box to reveal a folded piece of vermillion textile, *minsa*.

Kinjo-san shared that the *minsa* was a gift of love and protection from her mother to her father. The best-known *minsa* came from the Yaeyama Islands, a group of islands south of Okinawa's main island.

"You see this pattern here. It means long love."

Lynn carefully observed the vermillion textile. It had shades of yellow ochres and tangerines running across the tiny knots of red. She touched the alternating pattern of five and four small rectangles.

"Just before the war reached Okinawa, *chichi* buried the *minsa* deep in the soil, somewhere behind this house. He was afraid to damage it. Ha! And then, when the Americans came, a Yamato soldier gave him a hand grenade. He took the hand grenade and me into the caves to hide from the air raids. One night, he put me to bed and pulled the hand grenade."

As Kinjo-san closed the wooden box and put it away, Lynn made a promise to herself to not ask for stories unless Kinjo-san volunteered to share.

6.

October 2019

Shuri, Okinawa

Like a floating boat on a calm lake, the crescent moon hung quietly in the night sky. It cast a gentle light over Shuri Castle with just enough illumination and warmth. Yet, within seconds, winds and clouds moved in, concealing the moon from sight, turning those unexpected moments into memories.

It was Lynn's last night in Okinawa. Kinjo-san and Lynn were unable to find the right words to speak to one another. They had a quiet dinner together, and for the first time, they could hear the reports from the broadcasters on tv.

When dinner was over, Lynn volunteered to clean up and busied herself washing the dishes in the kitchen when she heard a loud shriek from Kinjo-san. She rushed out to the tatami room where Kinjo-san was. Mouth agape with soap water still dripping from her hands, she saw the main hall of Shuri Castle engulfed in flames on the television.

The news reported about the strong winds and electricity that caused the fire. But Lynn could make no further deductions from the information. By now, Kinjo-san was crying. Lynn put her arms around Kinjo-san and tried her best to comfort her.

Lynn did not remember how long she sat in the tatami room with Kinjo-san. They watched the venomous flames, strengthened by the strong winds of the night, burn through the surfaces of the castle walls. Like a sleeping giant set ablaze by a vengeful fire snake, roaring in pain as the fire cut through his flesh, revealing for all to see the shadows of his skeleton. It was his final act of death.

They followed the news until it reported no more of the castle. Just after that, Kinjo-san began to run a fever. By daybreak, Lynn was making her way to the pharmacy for medicine. On the streets, the mood was heavy and somber, people in funeral wear were making their way to the burning castle. A few families, hand-in-hand with their little ones, were headed that way too. They wanted to pay their final respects.

Back in Kinjo-san's place, Lynn tried her best to care for Kinjo-san. It would take Kinjo-san three days for her fever to subside, and another week before Kinjo-san could climb out of bed.

When Kinjo-san regained some strength, she put on a long black dress and walked with Lynn to the lake by the castle. The pair stood still silently. The once proud and dignified brick-red architectural emblem was now nothing more than a pile of burnt remains with large swirls of impenetrable black smoke rising from it. And though Lynn was a visitor to this foreign land, she felt emotional. She hugged Kinjo-san. Like a daughter who lost her father, Kinjo-san hugged Lynn back and cried in her arms.

7.

December 2019

Shuri, Okinawa

Okinawa's winter was easy. On a day in early December, it was just about sixty-eight Fahrenheit. Unexpectedly, or perhaps expectedly, after exploring the Chinese world as deeply as Lynn could, her initial spontaneous sprint out of it has her exploring a world, a culture at the periphery of it, so deeply intertwined and influenced by the Chinese, yet so uniquely independent of it.

She was impelled to travel to seek something. As a third-generation Singaporean Chinese, she was brought up to speak Chinese and held customs and beliefs from the Chinese system. Yet, she knew very little of the Chinese, or should she say, she did not know the shape and texture of the bones beneath her yellow skin and black hair. It never really bothered Lynn, though she was acutely aware of her unknowing until she grew older and finished school.

Yet, there was this restlessness, this gaping hole that appeared one day, and she felt it more and more as time passed. Lynn couldn't point a finger at it until her grandmother passed one day, and she dreamt of grandma's younger self waving goodbye to her. She wore a white cotton qipao, and uncannily, like how Lynn used to wear her hair at her age, she had her fringe pinned up to the side. Lynn's grandmother looked at Lynn. Lynn looked like her. That semblance of their youths was striking, even in a blurry dream state. When Lynn woke up, she was crying. She knew then she was a descendant of those who have left their ancestral birth grounds to form floating diasporas across the world. She knew then that she had two umbilical cords. She knew one well, but she barely knew the other, and she had to seek it out, her subconscious umbilical cord, the one in her blood past.

And so, Lynn packed a bag and left home. She started in Beijing and went through all the major cities and sites in the Chinese world until she could tell apart the Chinese of one region from another. Along the way, she met many interesting people traveling through

China. Some traveled to seek regardless of nationality or ethnicity, while others traveled to flee from something back home. Many traveled to both seek and flee.

Lynn was physically and emotionally exhausted when she reached Xiamen, Fujian. She got on a ferry to Gulangyu, a quaint island off the coast of Xiamen, and stayed quietly there for a couple of weeks. It was time to leave China and go somewhere new. Yet, after almost half a year in Okinawa, she finally learned that she has not really left the Chinese world after all.

One day, Kinjo-san chanced upon Lynn, cleaning the tiny photo frame with a painting of a woman in a faded pink *hanfu*, and said, almost carelessly, "That's the Moon Princess from China."

Lynn wasn't sure if the Moon Princess was a melancholic story or Kinjo-san was still sad about the castle fire. With care, Lynn beckoned Kinjo-san to tell her more. Kinjo-san sat next to Lynn and took the tiny photo frame in her hand; she tugged a small latch and opened the bi-fold frame to reveal a hidden painting of the Moon Princess in a hibiscus red and orange flower-patterned *ryusou*. She had her hair bunned up like the shape of a spiral shell, fastened from the back to the front with a long gold hairpin. She looked dignified and solemn with her half-smiling expression.

Kinjo-san continued, "There was a war, and her dynasty fell. With the help of magical creatures and the Flaming Pearl, she fled China and came here. My grandmother used to tell me that because we are her children, we will forever be blessed by her and the Flaming Pearl to live long and wrinkled."

8.

January 2020

Shuri, Okinawa

The coronavirus swept the world, and everything changed. One by one, like dominos falling to the earth, international borders, stadiums, schools, offices, shopping malls, cinemas, theaters, everything closed. The virus attacked congregations the worst, so even places of worship had to be closed. Nowhere was safe, yet the world found itself at home. It felt like the world was forced to power down. Except for the hospitals, they became battlegrounds. It was strange and uncomfortable. A world with no festivity or events. Even funerals were hastened to limit exposure.

Lynn could no longer travel, yet she did not want to go home. She was craving an adventure. There was something about Kinjo-san and her stories that compelled her to stay. Admittedly, she found herself growing attached to Kinjo-san. And so, she enrolled herself in language classes at a Japanese language school. Soon after, her student visa would be approved.

Kinjo-san was a lot better, both emotionally and physically. Lynn learned that the Shuri Castle had a special and sacred place in the Okinawans' hearts. It was a proud symbol of their legacy and heritage as children of the land.

One evening during dinner at Kinjo-san's place, Kinjo-san said, "The castle will be rebuilt, again."

"Again?"

"This isn't the first time it has been burnt down. It was horrible after the war. In the past, two Ryukyuan princes fought for the throne and burnt down the castle too. It will be fine. It has the Pearl."

"You mean the Flaming Pearl?"

Kinjo-san gave an unexpected sly smile, "You have been paying attention."

"Isn't the Flaming Pearl with the Moon Princess?"

"Yes, it was. But it eventually fell in the hands of a Ryukyuan prince who became King."

"What is the Flaming Pearl? Is it from China?"

"Nah, it is not from China. The Flaming Pearl came from The Ancients before countries and kingdoms formed. It went through many hands over the ages.

The emblem of the powerful phoenix, sometimes men, but usually it finds itself in female hands."

"What does it do?"

"It keeps you safe, very safe."

"But… if it keeps a person safe, and if it is with the castle, why did the castle burn down?"

At this point, Kinjo-san smiled again, "The Pearl is beyond life and death. The castle burnt down, but it will rise from its ashes again!"

Lynn nodded knowingly but was completely unconvinced.

"You don't believe me? Let me show you. Tonight, we go to the castle grounds."

9.

Kinjo-san was not joking about going to Shuri Castle. She prepared dinner for Lynn and herself, showered, and got ready. They left her place just before ten when the half-moon hung high in the cloudless sky. Lynn followed her slow but steady footsteps up the long five-hundred-year-old stone steps that led to the castle grounds. As there were only a few lamp posts lighting their way, they had to make do with torchlights. Thankfully, it was not a cold night, and they had a pleasant walk. It felt like a night pilgrimage with a good amount of uncertainty.

They reached the gardens surrounding the castle. Carefully placed yellow lights shone on the flowing curves of the slanting stone walls. They felt like ocean waves of the past, greeting them as they stepped deeper into a time bygone. They made their way to the tower gates. Expectedly, it was cordoned off with tapes and signage. Kinjo-san stared at it solemnly. Lynn tried her best to console Kinjo-san, "I mean, after all, it is a UNESCO Heritage Site, and the castle buildings burnt down just last year…"

"Follow me."

Lynn was surprised. She wondered if Kinjo-san was going to break in. What if they got caught?

Kinjo-san walked away from the main gate and made a left turn back to the castle gardens. She walked up to a pair of wooden gates with stout stone walls and a curved roof. They led to nowhere. They were conspicuous, large, clearly historical, a remnant of something. It was the first time Lynn saw the gates and she wondered how she could have missed seeing them in daylight when she first toured here.

Just beneath the stone steps fronting the gates, Kinjo-san kneeled and said a prayer. Lynn followed suit. And then, she got up and walked toward the gates.

"Kinjo-san, there's a lock on the gates-"

Yet, Kinjo-san pushed the gates, and they opened. She flashed Lynn a grin.

"Let's take a walk."

They went through the gates with Kinjo-san's lead and found themselves in a cold, damp, dark place. Lynn turned on her torchlight. They were in a cave. Kinjo-san kept walking straight, slowly but surely; a light shone into the cave from the entrance. They walked out of the cave, and Lynn found herself surrounded by tall, wavy mountains with an ocean bay in front of her. The sun was up in the sky; the waters were a glistering kerama blue. The duo stepped into the waters and walked. They barely came up to their knees and were just the right temperature. They were so clear that Lynn could see everything underneath. They were crossing the bay with their feet.

In awe, Lynn exclaimed, "I must be in a dream."

The next thing she knew, they were standing in its center. Kinjo-san looked around, took in the scenery, and smiled. And then, she looked into the waters. A glowing red pearl, the size of a fish ball, was resting on the sand.

"Pick it up."

Lynn bent her knees, placed her hand into the waters, and reached for the legendary Pearl. Serendipitously, a gush of energy surged into her. Lynn gasped and fell into the water. That was the first time she felt the birth of time, of all who came before her. It was also the first time she touched the souls of all whom the Pearl had touched.

10.

"Kinjo-san! I swear I felt the Pearl in my hand! But a second later, it was gone!"

With one ear listening to Lynn and the other paying attention to the sounds of the *fu champuru* frying in the wok, Kinjo-san barely gave a response but a little grin at the corner of her lips.

"Where did the Pearl go? Can we go back to that magical ocean place again?"

Kinjo-san paused her cooking and replied firmly, "No."

"Why?"

"It'll be a waste of time."

"No, it won't!"

"Yes, it will."

"Why would it be a waste of time?"

"Because you will not find the Pearl."

"Why not?"

"Because you are obsessed with it."

"That doesn't make sense!"

"The Pearl seeks you; you do not seek the Pearl."

"But last night, we went seeking the Pearl."

"That's not seeking."

Lynn stared at Kinjo-san in disbelief, who was enjoying every bite of her *fu champuru*.

"Don't believe me? Go try it yourself."

"I will."

That night, Lynn went to the castle grounds on her own. She walked up to the wooden gates, kneeled, and said a prayer. And then, she got up and pushed the gates. They would not open. She tried a few more times until they finally cracked open. She went in, but instead of finding herself in the cave leading to the magical ocean, she found herself tumbling down the heavy vegetation of the castle grounds.

metaland

1.

Seven minutes left. Amy stared into the water, her body grazing the surfaces of the bathtub. She was floating, but barely as she looked up at the digital clock on the wall:

23:23:00

10.08.2063

Never one to waste a second, she closed her eyes and slipped entirely into the water, anxious to feel weightless. Yet, like the amniotic sac of fluid that carried a child to her mother, all that sprang to her mind were the day's flashbacks of her mother's avatar in Metaland, the most sophisticated virtual reality universe. Her mother's avatar was set at her age thirty form, and her alluring presence evoked every floral note and beautiful blooms. Scents. Not something Amy liked in the metaverse. They were disarming to her. She remembered the anxious-inducing hug; the change of mood when her mother realized she was working for Sosi Pharma; the theatrical burst of flames.

It was the twenty-fifth trial. The twenty-fifth time Amy was with her mother in the metaverse. And yet, no progress in understanding the red orb, with zero clue on what to do next. She thought of her mother's cold, frail body in Sosi Lab. And she felt time behaving like the merciless night tides washing away a ship from shore to the disappearing horizon.

She had to steel herself. How could she convince her to speak of the red orb? Or as her mother called it, the Flaming Pearl. Then Amy remembered her mother jumping onto a fire-spitting dragon's neck and staring down at her with angry tears.

"Send my body back to the hospital! I will not have anything to do with Sosi!"

With that, the dragon and her mother vanished.

Short of air, Amy pushed herself out of the tub and struggled like a fish out of water.

She did not feel strong, and she did not know what to do.

2.

Eight Months Ago

Dr. Kim's clinic was painted a calming blue, her furniture and decorations in a neutral color palette. And then, there was that signature pop of a magenta table lamp next to her seat. She smiled a gentle smile, eyes indiscernible of her thoughts. Amy fidgeted in her seat like the schoolgirl she once was. She knew by now it was Dr. Kim's way of prompting her to carry on with her speaking. She still felt self-conscious in front of Dr. Kim, but she was willing to share.

"The last time we spoke was when I was twenty-five. I went home during the holidays, and we fought. Nothing new there. I packed my bags and left. My mom wasn't at my graduation either when I got my Ph.D. So you can imagine how unexpected it was when I saw her case file on my desk last week."

Dr. Kim put her pen down and smiled at Amy. The sort of smile you would expect from a proud mother to her beloved child.

"This is the first time, without my initiation, you choose to share about your mother."

Amy could feel her face and ears flushing red. She gave a feeble smile and said, "I don't know what to do."

"When you think of your mother, what comes to your mind?"

"A horse comes to my mind."

"A horse?"

"Yes, a free-spirited horse, running ecstatically on the Mongolian steppes, running with the wind, hair in her face, without a care in the world."

"That's nice. She sounds very carefree."

"She was. She was eccentric and very intuitive. Very sharp, too. Perhaps it was her gift or quality she honed from her travels. She could see through trickery and illusions in a heartbeat. I could not keep a lie from her."

"How does that make you feel?"

"I felt powerless."

"Powerless?"

"Yes, powerless. She was kind, so kind to everyone she met. People loved her. People loved her even more when they experienced her stories in Oki Times.

"The world she created?"

"Yes, in Metaland. Her stories were so different, so unexpected. They caught people off guard, and people liked that. I did share previously that she was a Genesis 0. She was famous for her fantasy stories, but to her those stories were true."

"Tell me more about these stories."

"I'm not sure where to start. There's so many of them."

"How does it feel to see your mother now?"

"I still feel powerless."

"But your mother is in a coma now."

"I know."

3.

The next day, Timothy was in Amy's office. In silence, barely making eye contact, they were waiting for the other person to initiate.

He looked at the engraved nameplate on her desk:

CHANG MIN CHU, AMY

Finally, without raising his eyes, he said, "Professor Chang, I'm here to speak to you about the comatose patient."

Timothy was no more qualified than Amy was, but he was better with people, and he had the right pedigree within the organization.

"What about it, Professor Lim?"

"I'm sure you understand, you have been in our star department as long as I have. We cannot allow such a protracted case, especially one that requires so much of our manpower and resources."

Amy nodded her head in feigned understanding. Timothy was no longer a scientist or a friend; he had become a bureaucrat. Perhaps he was always a bureaucrat.

"Management is pressing. You know what that means."

"If I may, I would like to put up a case for one more trial."

"You do know we have done twenty-five trials, right? A first for our department."

"Yes, I'm fully aware of that, and I would like to put up a case for one more."

"I made the appeal myself to management to have you lead this case because you are the best in the field."

"Thank you, I'm deeply flattered."

"Given your relationship with the patient, there is clearly a conflict of interest… So don't mess it up."

Amy's mother was the first human in a coma to be plugged into the metaverse. They discovered that deep in the recesses of her unconscious mind, there was still a conscious mind or, in Amy's contemplations, a soul. It could be brought to the surface, spoken to, in the metaverse. However, they learned too that experiences in the metaverse of a comatose human did not form memories. Her mother had no memory of her previous plays in Metaland. In other words, each time her mother entered the metaverse, it was like a fresh new player all over again.

"We need more breakthroughs and faster. Else, we'll have to force one."

"Force a breakthrough?"

Timothy's eyes softened. Amy was caught off guard.

"As you are already aware, the patient was brought in here because of the stories she created in the metaverse. At the heart of her make-believe worlds and characters is the red orb, or as she termed it, 'the Flaming Pearl.' The red orb is the key to cellular regeneration, rebirth, 'rising from the ashes' or so is the hypothesis we need to prove. The patient needs to tell us exactly where the red orb is in the physical world or how it can be made, else-"

Timothy halted in his tracks and hesitated as though he ate something foul and could not speak of it. After looking away from Amy's nameplate, he finally continued, "we would have to administer Anticreatine on the patient."

"You can't. That drug is still undergoing clinical trials."

"This qualifies for an exemption."

"You can't. The drug may kill her. We don't know, it has never been done before! We need to run more tests."

"I have approval."

"On what grounds?"

"Exceptional medical improvement."

Amy's lips quivered. On what grounds for medical improvement? She ran through everything she knew about the situation and the drug. She held onto all the science, observations, and knowledge that she knew. And she understood right before Timothy explained.

"Anticreatine was invented to bring everyone back into the metaverse. It quiets the neurochemical change of brain cells to not enter 'creation mode.' When the brain isn't in 'creation mode,' it cannot go into hyper-drive. Nor does it enter into a metaverse-induced delirium and receive all the negative stuff that comes with the metaverse. The brain retains all its other functions- memory, processing, decision-making, etc. It is less apt to create new thoughts, feelings, and actions. Hence, management would like to see if Anticreatine can 'quieten the active mind of the patient.' By doing so, convincing it to regurgitate everything it knows about the red orb."

"How do you know what she created was even true? She's a Genesis 0! They create the most fantastical worlds in the metaverse. Yet, they're known to be highly deceptive too."

Amy did not even believe in her words. Those were words of emotional Amy; not the words of Professor Chang.

Timothy smiled and said, "You know as well as I do that everything in the metaverse is almost fictional and that every creation stems from something accurate and factual. This organization was built out of stories from the metaverse. Stories that were distilled, crystallized into their truths, tested, and built out. That's how we have the empathy drug, the sonic hearing aids, the superfruits, and now, we're on our way to having the rebirth drug."

How could Amy argue against this? Dreams that turn into reality. Imaginations that propel the advancement of humanity.

"Amy, I know this is hard, but pause for a moment and consider what this will mean for us, our department, to develop the rebirth drug. The patient only has a one percent chance of waking up, you know this. And you know what this means. With or without administering Anticreatine, her legacy to this world-"

"Give me one more trial. I will get the patient to open up about the red orb."

"Fine, but then we proceed with Anticreatine."

"Thank you."

4.

Amy walked into the room half an hour early. Everyone involved in the trial was already there making their final checks. Timothy was there too. Beneath the front of professionalism, she could sense a mix of sympathy, ambivalence, and mostly frustration from her colleagues. Timothy was right. People were unhappy. People wanted to move on to other patients. How could she blame them? They were like the nurse bees in the hive; only potential queen bees came to their team of neuroscientists, psychologists, doctors, and interpreters. They selected and nursed the best. With her mother's case taking up eight months of their time, they had lost many potential queen bees.

Amy's mother was seated on one of the two chairs with a blanket over her. Her face wrinkled and lifeless. Amy kneeled by her side. Careful not to disturb her ventilator, for the first time in thirteen years, she held both of her mother's hands.

"Ma, I know you're in there. Listen, you have to tell me everything you know about the red orb. You know, the time you used the V-Skin GX and created a red orb in Metaland. I was twenty-two then. You told me how amazing the experience was and that everyone loved it. But I was so angry with you, so angry at your betrayal of not keeping your promise. Why did you fixate on the red orb, the 'Flaming Pearl' as you called it?"

"Ma. Tell me everything about the Pearl when we go in there later. I want to hear it. Tell me all those stories like you always did when I was growing up, about all those adventures you had when you were traveling the world. I want to hear it. I really do. If you don't, you are going to…"

At that moment, Amy could feel Timothy's eyes on her. She did not disclose everything she knew about the red orb to him after all.

She had nothing more to say. She walked to her seat and downed a glass of water. She grabbed the lightweight headwear with the words "V-Skin GX" printed on its side. She tapped it on and placed it on her head. A white light grew from the darkness. A soft hum and the aroma of freshly brewed coffee filled the air.

An angelic voice spoke, "Hi Professor Chang, welcome back to Blackbox 61 of Sosi Labs. Shall we pick up from where we left?"

Amy replied, "Log in a new case file, please. Name it 'Oki Times'."

"New case file, 'Oki Times,' created."

And then, Amy imagined her childhood home, the olive-green walls, the white wooden stairs, and the warm orange furniture. The colorful carpets and rugs and the smell of fresh tropical spices hung in the kitchen. The background piano played, and her tall, lean father, Benny, was making tea, as he always had.

On this day, a sudden and ceaseless storm appeared.

These thoughts, her imagination, came to life in the metaverse. She took her seat on the well-worn orange sofa. With a thought, she transformed her avatar-self into her nine-year-old self and waited patiently for her mother to come home.

5.

The key turned and the door opened. Lynn walked in, visibly confused. Benny looked up, smiled warmly at Lynn, and continued making his tea. While Lynn looked at Benny, then Amy, and then the house she knew to be home. Upon which, Amy ran up from the orange sofa and hugged Lynn.

"Mama! You're home. Where did you go this time? Tell me, please!"

Lynn thought for a moment, yet nothing came to her mind.

Benny chided her, "Didn't you go to Okinawa again?"

Lynn nodded her head slowly and said, "Yes…"

"Where did you go in Okinawa this time? Tell me!"

Lynn got excited. The smell of Kinjo-san's antiques permeated the room. She replied, "Oh, you want to know? I went to visit Kinjo-san, of course! She can barely leave the house. But she is in good spirits."

"What did you do in Kinjo-san's house!"

"Oh, the usual! We talked and talked. Ate and ate."

"What stories did she share with you this time?"

A large wooden box appeared by the orange sofa. Before Amy could react, Lynn looked at the box and frowned. Was that Kinjo-san's box she just saw? Yet, the wooden box was no longer there in a blink of an eye. Benny placed a hot cup of tea in front of her and sat next to her.

"Mama, what stories did Kinjo-san tell you this time?"

Lynn sipped her green tea slowly. This was unexpected. Amy was never interested in Kinjo-san's stories. Especially since they were always the same to her.

The young Amy asked again, "Mama, what stories did Kinjo-san tell you this time?"

Lynn thought for a second, but she could not remember the details of her trip. Something was amiss, yet she couldn't put a finger to it. She observed the interiors of her home and then Benny and Amy. Benny was Benny and not Benny at the same time. So was Amy. She stared at the orange clock on the wall. The soft yet persistent ticking sound of the clock's hand filled the space. Without losing sight of the wall clock, she asked, "What day is today, Amy?"

"Sunday, Mama."

Lynn stared at her with a frown. It was Thursday when she got home, weary from her trip to the museum, and before she knew it, her eyes closed, and she drifted into sleep.

"What do you want to know, sweetie?"

"Well, tell me something you have never shared before!"

This was not the Amy she knew. Where was Amy? Who was this Benny in front of her? Her mind raced. All of a sudden, she could hear the raging storm outside. There could only be a few possibilities for all these to happen, and worst of all, she smelled an illusion. She composed herself quickly, considered her options, and decided to play along. She decided to share a particular memory of Kinjo-san. She was ready to set the place ablaze.

6.

Lynn sat down and spoke of the time when she first visited Okinawa. She talked about touring the castle, meeting Kinjo-san and attempting to catch a black butterfly with her, cleaning Kinjo-san's antiques, and listening to plenty of fascinating family stories. When she spoke, her eyes lit up. She captivated everyone easily, even without the theatrics or illusions one can conjure up in the metaverse. She continued to share with Benny and Amy her trip to the medicine hall with Kinjo-san and the day Kinjo-san developed a fever. It was a day of anguish as the pair witnessed the burning of the castle on television. It was a story Lynn had never shared before, which surprised Amy. Lynn recounted every detail of the burning castle. She drew her audience in, including those observing them on screens. To the point that not a single one of them noticed the kitchen stove catching fire.

The fire spread to the wooden cabinets and walls and then onto the main door. It continued to spread until it surrounded the trio. Lynn made no attempt to acknowledge the fire and continued her storytelling. Finally, the fire moved in and trapped Lynn. Amy screamed but Lynn barely flinched. Amy directed massive gallons of running water from the taps and showerhead to the flames, and within seconds, she put out the fire.

Amy spoke with her adult voice, "What were you thinking!"

Lynn yelled back, "I knew it! I knew it!"

"You could have gotten hurt!"

"My brain would only be tricked to feel pain on my skin and flesh. But this! What is all this?"

Lynn looked at the house with broken furniture, burnt wood, soot, and smoke. She looked at Benny and then at Amy. Amy transformed back to her adult self and waved for Benny to go.

"Why are we here?"

Amy thought for some time. This was her last chance with Lynn, and she had to make it work. She had to.

"Ma, I'm… sorry."

A long silence fell between them.

"I don't know what else to do. This is the only way."

"What are you talking about?"

"Ma, I know I was angry with you, angry with everything, and I left."

Lynn slowly sat back down. She did not feel so strong anymore. She spoke slowly, "I know you were angry. Angry and hurt. I regret it very much too."

Amy sat next to Lynn and buried her face in her hands. She composed herself and said, "Ma, I need you to trust me. We don't have time to talk about it now, but I want to make this right for others."

Lynn looked weary and asked feebly, "What do you need?"

"I need you to tell me everything you know about the Flaming Pearl."

"The Pearl seeks you; you do not seek the Pearl."

"Tell me from the beginning. Every detail. I need to know."

"You will not find the Pearl."

"I need to at least try."

Lynn nodded her head in understanding. She walked to the main door and beckoned for Amy to follow. As she opened it, they stepped into Lynn's youth, at a time when she first met Kinjo-san in Okinawa.

the shimmering moon
on howling nights

echoes from an island

alicia ang

night shadow

Quietness is the stone-cold castle ruin at night.
Watch out for island snakes hidden in tall bushes.
They kill with one bite.

Now see those two shadows play
in a hot summer May.
Dancing in a chase, those precious days.
Sweetness of youth, never here to stay.

No, see those after-rain glisters?
The smell of this powerhouse still lingers.

Deep in the night,
I hear grand processions drum me by.
Trumpets at the gate cry,
haunting ritual chants,
even anguish war cries.

Wake up.
Those worlds
have long gone by.

The crickets cry, they do cry.
Clowders of cat eye me goodbye.
They're the masters now of these walls and sky.

See that parallel world in the distance-
just two shadows strolling by
the castle walls.

There they are now-

under the sprawling gajumaru tree,
checking off their dreams,
all pieces and in-betweens.
Their own king and queen.

I have a fear that I will forget

I have a fear that I will forget.
Who am I without my memories?

There is nothing on the island,
nothing concrete.
The winds call the tune.
They sway the sands and the hearts,
and we wonder why there's nothing here.
And so, I dragged a boat by hand.
With tears flowing down the river,
I rowed and rowed and left my island behind.

parting words

∞

echoes from an island

alicia ang

dreaming of a fish

Wheezing in mid-air,
she thrashed herself
from side to side.

As if such a vigorous response
will pull in the life essence that
she needs.

The hook loosens,
she bolts into the water.

Fresh air in her body,
she finds herself
awake once more.

three

It's the cat's supper time.
The ever-growing kitten,
feasting on her Italian pumpkin and salmon,
you can say food is her long-standing passion.

The boyfriend savors his
coffee pudding with chocolate drizzle.
7-Eleven's latest treat for her
stream of unwavering patrons.

The water simmers.
A warm brew of spice tea
will do for me tonight.

Time turns in circles anon.
This moment, a flurry of activity.
All at once, each at its own,
in this space of time.

what do you seek?

I am from the city, a famous one.
Since I was a little girl,
I see people from hometowns near and afar
flocking to my vicinity.
What is it that they seek?
Why do they want to be where I am?

Did they come to see the sky-high skyscrapers?
Or is it the world cuisines and sensational cocktails
that tantalize their tongues and souls?
They can't be here for the competition, crowds,
or congestion.
Can they *really* stand the city noise, little pride,
and inflation?

I wonder if they have found what they seek
in my place called home.

I noticed there seems to be a sense of shame
coming from anywhere less than a sparkling city,
or a place to go on a travel map.
What is it that I have that they don't?
Am I so blinded by my privilege that
I don't know *life*?

I learned in school that most of the world lives in cities,
for they capture our imagination and spirit.
Not to mention the lure of
opportunity, variety, convenience, and thrill!
Like school kids with their test scores,
do you know that cities are ranked?
In the game of life,
do city-dwellers have the upper hand?

Sometimes I say a quiet prayer at night.
I don't understand many things.

I learned that our world of peace
touches not the troubled corners of the world.
Yet, as we sip hot lattes in our mornings,
they appear in our news and Twitter feed.

Redressed as low-wage workers,

so close amongst us,

yet, barely seen.

It is not just about the physical world.

We are in a digital divide too.

Invisible walls of spaces that are rarified by bandwidth.

I know something that you don't know,

and you have no way to access it.

When can they ever hold keys to blockchain addresses?

They who will always have two worlds

or more in their hearts.

I feel like a hypocrite.

I know peace is built upon flesh and swords

and that I descend from

bloodlines of war-winning tribes.

Were they noble wars that were fought?

I will never know.

Who trusts history now?

There was no social media then, then, and then!

∞

Since a long time ago,
I knew I wanted to leave my city.
I can't find what I seek in there.
Not in any street or alley.
Many a time, I told myself,
"Maybe it is just a feeling."
Yet, I feel it growing in my being.
What if I really go out there and seek?
What if I don't find what I want?
What if I go back empty-handed?

I looked at the portrait of the waves and the ocean
that I hung on my wall.
They call to me, first quietly, gently,
and then, loudly and incessantly.
One day, they drowned out my fears,
and flooded me with the courage to leave my city.

Not for good.
But yes, I left in search of something
until I see it out of my window,
until I feel it in me.

And I wonder now,
they who left their homes to go to my city,
do they feel what I feel now?
Is it in us to seek the treasures of life?

Some of us are forced to seek,
some of us have the option to seek.
Of that that we seek,
some of which need the courage to be found,
some of which need surrender to be realized
that we had them all along.

I found it.
I can't believe it!
I found it.

Tell me something now,
what do you seek?
Will you create space for yourself to find it?
Will you shed tears and sweat over it?

Like breathing,
will you live to seek it?

about the author

Alicia Ang is a Singaporean author, marketeer, and interpreter. With a Beijing Government Municipal Scholarship, she studied International Politics with a minor in Art at Peking University. Unexpectedly, she found compelling stories to share and learned that stories come to her when she travels. She then became a student writer with the largest Singaporean Chinese-language newspaper, *Lianhe Zaobao*. In 2013, she won Second Place in the 2nd China Original Short Musical Script Competition. Her debut collection of short stories and poems, *Echoes from an Island*, was published in 2023. She is currently in Okinawa, Japan, working on her next creation.

thealiciaang.com
@thealiciaang

acknowledgements

This journey would not have been possible without family, coaches, and friends, who provided me with unwavering love, advice, encouragement, and support. Special mentions to Mom, Dad, Alvin Ang, Masaru Sakai, Yeo Quan Yin, Liang Yong, Mandy Jeffery, and Yurie Jiroku.

And a big thank you to my wonderful Siamese-mixed furball, Coco. My writing ritual would forever remain incomplete without your companionship, pee smells, and chewing sounds.